PEOPLE POISONS

PROCESSED FOODS

BY

MIGNONNE GUNASEKARA

Cavendish Square
New York

Published in 2023 by Cavendish Square Publishing, LLC
29 East 21st Street
New York, NY 10010

Website: cavendishsq.com

Edited by: William Anthony

Designed by: Danielle Rippengill

Cataloging-in-Publication Data

Names: Gunasekara, Mignonne.
Title: Processed foods / Mignonne Gunasekara.
Description: New York : Cavendish Square, 2023. | Series: People poisons | Includes glossary and index.
Identifiers: ISBN 9781502663801 (pbk.) | ISBN 9781502663825 (library bound) | ISBN 9781502663818 (6 pack) | ISBN 9781502663832 (ebook)
Subjects: LCSH: Food industry and trade--Juvenile literature.
Classification: LCC TP370.3 G858 2023 | DDC 641.3--dc23

CPSIA compliance information: Batch #CSCSQ23: For further information contact Cavendish Square Publishing LLC, New York, New York, at 1-877-980-4450.

Printed in the United States of America

Image Credits

All images are courtesy of Shutterstock.com, unless otherwise specified. With thanks to Getty Images, Thinkstock Photo and iStockphoto. Cover: wow.subtropica, Rayyy, sokolovski, Milan M, Olga Miltsova, udra11. 4 – Jack Frog. 5 – Tomsickova Tatyana. 6 – Ahanov Michael. 7 – Vladimir Nenezic. 8 – luchschenF. 9 – Shestakoff. 10 – Niloo. 11 – Feng Yu. 12 – vystekimages. 13 – Stokkete. 14 – HandmadePictures. 15 – Ekaterina_Minaeva, Ron Dale. 16 – Africa Studio, Motortion Films. 17 – didesign021. 18 – junpinzon, Stephen McCluskey. 19 – Midhat. 20 – wavebreakmedia. 21 – EKramar. 22 – Elena Sherengovskaya, Hafiez Razali. 23 – Arayabandit, D. Pimborough, Moving Moment, MWPHOTOS55.

CONTENTS

Words that look like this can be found in the glossary on page 24.

TOO MUCH of a GOOD THING

Cooking is a great way to spend time with your loved ones.

We all need food to live. It gives us the strength to grow, run, and learn. It can also be tasty and fun!

However, there are certain types of foods that can be bad for us, especially if we eat them a lot. What happens to our bodies when we eat these foods?

Some **ingredients** and ways of cooking can make food less healthy.

What Is PROCESSED FOOD?

Processed food is any food that has been changed from the way it is found in nature. Any food that isn't processed is raw.

Freezing, canning, and drying are all ways of processing food.

Processing food can be very helpful. It can help keep food fresh so we waste less of it.

Not all processed foods are bad. We just need to watch out for the unhealthy ingredients and ways of cooking that processing foods can bring.

ADDITIVES

Additives can be natural or human-made.

Additives are ingredients that can be added to food as it is processed. Some additives give the food certain flavors or colors, and some make the food last longer.

Some additives hold food together, almost like glue. These kinds of additives might be used in some types of ice cream. Other additives can make food tastier.

PRESERVATIVES

Additives that make food last longer are called preservatives. Preservatives allow food to be moved all over the world without going bad.

Have you ever seen expiration dates on food packages?

An expiration date can also be called a "use by" date or a "best before" date.

This date tells us when the food is no longer safe to eat. With the help of preservatives, the expiration date can be much later than normal.

BADDITIVES

Some people can be sensitive to additives.

This means they might have a bad **reaction** to them. They may get an upset stomach or **hives** if they eat food with certain additives in them.

People who are sensitive to some additives need to carefully read food packaging. This helps them stay away from foods that use those additives.

In most countries, packaging must say which additives are in the food.

INGREDIENTS to WATCH OUT For

Some ingredients can lead to health problems if we eat too much of them. A little bit of salt, sugar, or fat is fine, but how do we check if we are eating too much of them?

Many countries around the world use colors on the packaging to show the amount of salt, sugar, and fat in the food. This is a quick, easy way to check how healthy the food is.

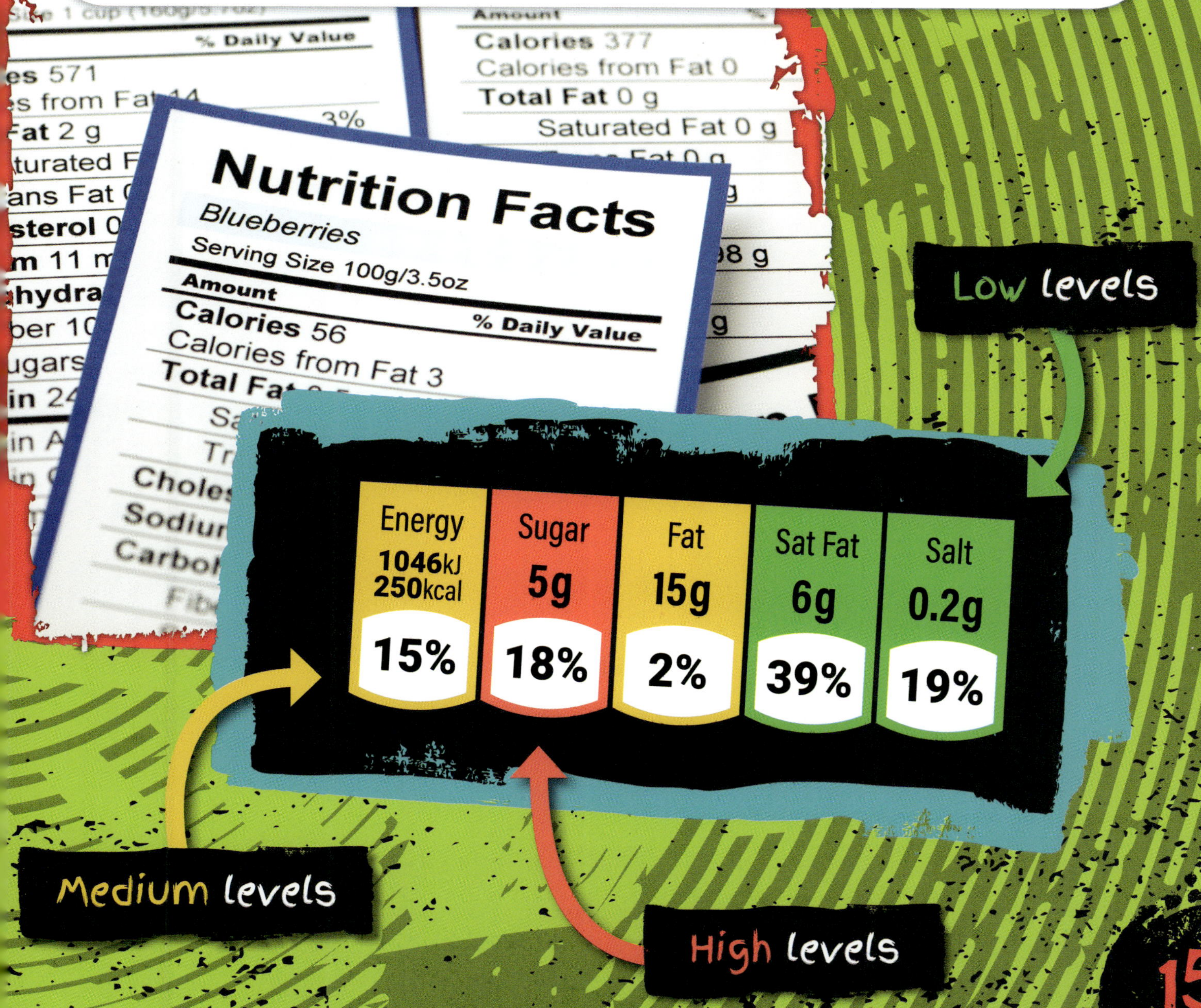

Sugar and salt are used to make food taste better. You shouldn't worry about eating a little of these things. However, eating too much of them can be bad for you.

Salt and sugar are often found in foods such as pizza or chocolate.

Children aged four to six should have less than 19 grams of sugar and 2 grams of salt a day.

Eating too much sugar could lead to **tooth decay** or health problems. Too much salt could cause **heart disease** later in life.

UNHEALTHY COOKING

Some ways of cooking can make foods unhealthy. Here are some of those ways.

Frying in oil

Boiling vegetables too much is not good. They lose a lot of their **nutrients** in the water.

Deep fat frying is one of the unhealthiest ways of cooking food. Fries, doughnuts, and chicken are often deep fried.

A HEALTHY Diet

Meals should have a **starchy** food, such as potatoes, pasta, rice, or bread.

A healthy diet might include some beans, eggs, meat, or fish.

For a healthy diet, you must eat lots of different types of foods. Make sure you eat five **portions** of fruit and vegetables each day.

Eating fresh food is very healthy for us. Cooking it in a healthy way is also important. For example, steaming vegetables is very healthy.

Vegetables in a steamer

FOOD SWAPS

Here are some foods you can swap to have a healthier diet.

Have low-fat milk instead of whole-fat milk.

If you want something sweet and sugary, have some fruit instead.

Hot dogs and pizza have lots of bad fat. Avocado, fish, and seeds are full of good fat.

Have plain yogurt with banana instead of a sugary yogurt.

For a snack, try some bread instead of chocolate.

Eat a **whole grain** cereal instead of a sugary cereal.

GLOSSARY

heart disease damage or illness that affects the heart
hives a red rash on the skin that itches a lot
ingredients foods that are mixed or cooked together to make a meal
nature everything in the world around us that was not made by humans
nutrients natural substances that plants and animals need to grow and stay healthy
portions the right amounts of food you should eat in one sitting
raw uncooked or unchanged
reaction in sickness, getting feelings of illness from something such as nuts
starchy full of lots of starch, which is a tasteless, white part of food from plants
tooth decay when teeth become rotten
whole grain contains the whole grain seed and all of the nutrients with nothing being removed

INDEX